SEXUAL HARASSMENT IN THE AGE OF #METOO

Crossing the Line

by Rebecca Stanborough

Consultant:
Louise Roth, Associate Professor of Sociology, University of Arizona

COMPASS POINT BOOKS
a capstone imprint

Compass Point Books are published by Capstone
1710 Roe Crest Drive, North Mankato, Minnesota 56003
www.capstonepub.com

Editorial Credits
Michelle Bisson, editor; Sarah Bennett, designer; Kelly Garvin, media researcher;
Katy LaVigne, production specialist

Photo Credits
AP Images/Skip Foreman, 27: Newscom: Everett Collection, 26, Jeff Malet
Photography, 5, Junfu Han/TNS, 23, KEVIN DIETSCH/UPI, 53, NTB/SCANPIX/
REUTERS, 52; Shutterstock: Antonio Guillem, 41, 48, Avivi Aharon, 17, Cube29,
cover, Daisy Daisy, 39, dnaveh, 51, ESB Professional, 50 (top), Everett Collection, 15,
7, 8, Jazzmany, 50 (bottom), Joaquin Corbalan P, 29, Joseph Sorrentino, 33, Kathy
Hutchins, 25 (top)(bottom inset), Rob Crandall, 10, 49, sezer66, 45

Design elements: Shutterstock: 21MARCH, Hybrid_Graphics

Library of Congress Cataloging-in-Publication Data
Names: Stanborough, Rebecca, author.
  Title: Sexual harassment in the age of #metoo : crossing the line / by
    Rebecca Stanborough.
  Description: North Mankato, Minn. : Compass Point Books, [2020] | Audience:
    Age: 10-12. | Audience: Grade 4 to 6.
  Identifiers: LCCN 2019001431| ISBN 9780756561710 (hardcover) | ISBN
    9780756562267 (pbk.) | ISBN 9780756561932 (ebook pdf)
  Subjects: LCSH: Sexual harassment—Juvenile literature. | Sexual harassment
    of women—Juvenile literature. | Sexual harassment of men—Juvenile
    literature.
  Classification: LCC HQ1237 .S823 2020 | DDC 305.42—dc23
  LC record available at https://lccn.loc.gov/2019001431

Printed and bound in the United States of America.
PA71

Table of Contents

CHAPTER ONE

What Is **Sexual** Harassment?

I went up a narrow set of stairs leading from the living room to a second floor to use the bathroom. When I got to the top of the stairs, I was pushed from behind into a bedroom. I couldn't see who pushed me. Brett and Mark came into the bedroom and locked the door behind them. There was music already playing in the bedroom. It was turned up louder by either Brett or Mark once we were in the room. I was pushed onto the bed and Brett got on top of me. He began running his hands over my body and grinding his hips into me. I yelled, hoping someone downstairs might hear me, and tried to get away from him, but his weight was heavy. . . . I thought that Brett was accidentally going to kill me.

—from the testimony of Dr. Christine Blasey-Ford, during the confirmation hearings for U.S. Supreme Court Justice Brett Kavanaugh

Clouds had been gathering all morning. By the time Dr. Christine Blasey-Ford began speaking to the Senate Judiciary Committee, a chilly autumn rain was falling. Inside the Dirksen Senate Building, Ford told a story familiar to many women in the U.S. and around the world. She spoke about a sexual assault she experienced while she was in high school. When she gave her statement, the members of the committee questioned her. Some of them were supportive. Some were angry. Nearby, on the rain-glazed steps of the U.S. Supreme Court building, crowds of supporters waved hand-lettered posters. They chanted, "We believe Christine."

Judge Brett Kavanaugh, the man Blasey-Ford accused, strongly denied ever assaulting anyone. His testimony convinced many on the Senate Judiciary Committee. Some of them said Blasey-Ford was motivated by politics. Others said her memory was too spotty to trust. Some believed Kavanaugh was an innocent man falsely accused. After an FBI investigation that lasted one week, Kavanaugh's nomination to the U.S. Supreme Court was confirmed.

The debate struck the nation at a crucial moment. For months, allegations of sexual assault had been in the headlines. Once-beloved comic Bill Cosby was on trial. He was accused of drugging and raping young women. Famed Hollywood producer Harvey Weinstein had been accused of demanding sexual acts from young female actors auditioning for film roles. And several male student athletes received little or no punishment for sexual assaults from judges worried about the boys' futures.

The nation was stirred up by what seemed like an epidemic of sexual assault. The problem was so widespread that people had begun simply saying #MeToo on social media to show that they had also experienced sexual harassment or assault.

But is sexual assault really that common? Is the #MeToo movement a sudden surge, or has sexual assault been part of our culture all along?

Fact

What exactly do we mean?

- **Sexual harassment** is any unwelcome sexual advance. It could be words, gestures, or touching.
- **Sexual assault** is touching another person's body in a sexual way without permission.
- **Rape culture** is when a society minimizes, tolerates, or normalizes sexual harassment and assault.

The History of Harassment

Sexual harassment has been around for centuries. Probably longer. It was part of the sordid history of slavery in the United States. Slaveowners regularly raped enslaved women—and even men. They felt entitled to use their bodies however they wanted. After all, these men and women were legally their property.

Enslaved women were auctioned off as though they were merchandise, not people. Their bodies were examined by men who might want to buy them.

Even after emancipation, the sexual abuse of black women continued. Men who employed housemaids took all sorts of liberties with their employees. The criminal justice system allowed white people to get away with lynching, or killing people, without a trial. It also would have denied justice to a woman who accused a white employer of rape.

As far back as the 1800s the Women's Christian Temperance Union waged a public battle against sexual abuse of women in all kinds of working environments. Sexual exploitation was rampant in every industry. Women of every color and background endured it. In

Helen Campbell's 1887 report on women wage earners, she documented the abuse of women in the clothing industry and in many other kinds of factory work.

Dominance, Not Desire

Some scholars have reasoned that the abuse of women was not about sexual desire. Instead, they argue, men wanted to keep women out of the workforce. By exposing women to threats and sexual attacks, they made the workplace dangerous. What woman would want to go to work if it meant putting up with such treatment?

In the early 1900s, many women worked in New York City's Garment District. The women had little space in which to work, and even less light or fresh air.

In that way, sexual harassment was part of a larger social system that denied equality to women. Many colleges and universities did not admit women until the 1900s. Women could not vote until 1920. And the job market limited women to the lowest-paying kinds of work.

Until the Civil Rights Act of 1964, there were no laws to protect women from workplace harassment. If a woman brought a complaint against her employer, it was her reputation and her job prospects that would be damaged. The court was rarely on her side. One 19th-century law paper said women had to show "utmost resistance" for a sexual encounter to be considered rape. She had to shout, bite, and strike with her hands and feet to defend herself. If a woman wanted to claim rape, there had to be "marks of violence" on her body.

1964: A Very Good Year

Then came Title VII of the Civil Rights Act of 1964. It made it unlawful to discriminate against people based on their sex, race, religion, and national origin. In the years following passage of the law, many workers sued to enforce their rights. The courts began to define what kinds of behaviors were not allowed at work.

The law also came to recognize two different kinds of sexual harassment. The first kind is called *quid pro quo*, which means "this for that." It describes situations where a person in power demands sexual behavior in exchange for something else—usually a job, raise, or promotion.

Anita Hill Takes a Stand

In 1991 Supreme Court Justice Thurgood
Marshall stepped down. President George
H.W. Bush nominated Clarence Thomas to
replace Marshall. Before he could be sworn in,
Thomas had to be confirmed by the Senate.
But there was a problem. A respected law
professor named Anita Hill shared details
of a troubling story about Thomas. Hill told
the FBI that Thomas had sexually harassed
her when they worked together at the Equal
Employment Opportunity Commission
(EEOC) in Oklahoma. That had been 10 years

earlier. It wasn't the first time Hill had told her story. She had told
coworkers and friends at the time. But now, Professor Hill felt she had to
tell those who were doing background checks on Thomas. She believed it
was her civic duty.

The Senate Judiciary Committee asked Hill to testify in Washington.
For eight hours, while cameras clicked and reporters scribbled, a panel of
all-white, all-male senators questioned her. Many, she felt, had already
made up their minds that she was lying. Thomas denied her allegations.
He compared the accusations to a "high-tech lynching." The committee
voted to support Thomas's nomination to the Court. The full Senate then
confirmed Thomas by a vote of 52–48.

After her testimony, Professor Hill was hounded by reporters. She
received death threats by mail. But for many Americans, Hill's testimony
was a triumph. They felt she had shed light on sexual harassment. If it
could happen at the EEOC to a woman as intelligent as Hill, many people
felt they had a chance of being believed. In the years following Hill's
testimony, official reports of sexual harassment skyrocketed.

The courts also recognize a second kind of harassment: hostile work environment. In this case, someone in your workplace makes you feel unsafe because they keep doing or saying sexual things to you or around you. For example, a coworker sends sexually explicit photos to you or makes sexual jokes around you even after you ask him to stop. A hostile work environment is far more common than quid pro quo.

Protections for LGBTQ People

Title VII of the Civil Rights Act bans sex discrimination but it doesn't clearly protect the rights of people who identify as LGBTQ. In 2017 the EEOC and three federal courts took the position that these rights extend to LGBTQ people. These courts have recognized that gender-based harassment can occur at work even if coworkers are the same gender. The courts have also decided that hostile work environments can be created by targeting people because of their sexual orientation or gender identity. But those courts have not had the final word. Sixteen states have appealed, and the case may soon go to the Supreme Court. They are asking that equal rights not be granted.

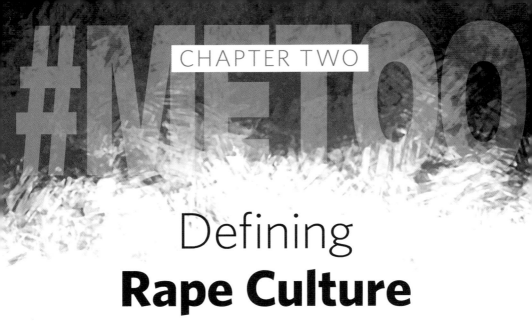

CHAPTER TWO

Defining
Rape Culture

The bell rings. Students pour into crowded hallways. As a boy passes a girl, he grabs her rear end. "Hey!" she says, slapping away his hand. He laughs and keeps walking. No matter how many times she reports him to the dean, nothing ever changes.

A trans student reaches into her gym locker to get her clothes. Someone slams into her, calls her an ugly name, and whispers, "You're going to hell."

After months of extra practice sessions, a coach tells a player how special she is. He kisses her and asks her not to tell. If she mentions the kiss, he says, she will destroy his career.

Sexual harassment and assault happen every day all over the world. They happen in hallways, bathrooms, gyms, clubs, offices, parks, and places of worship. One national survey showed that 81 percent of women have been sexually harassed online or in real life. It happens so often that sometimes it seems no one and no place is safe.

This can be especially painful if you are part of a group that is already vulnerable to other forms of discrimination. Women, LGBTQ people, people with disabilities, black and brown people, and people without much money usually have less power in our society. And they are all much more likely to be sexually assaulted.

Sexual violence is serious problem with deep roots in our culture. To fight it, we have to understand *why* it is so common.

Fact

When a society normalizes, tolerates, or minimizes sexual assault, it makes rape more likely to occur. That phenomenon is called rape culture.

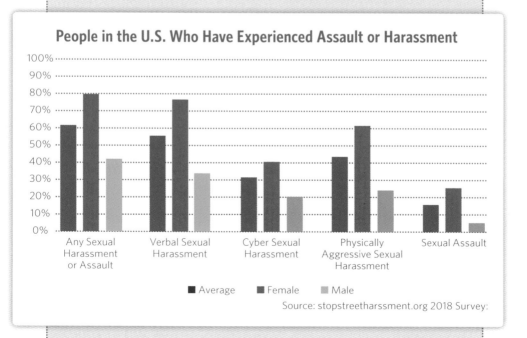

People in the U.S. Who Have Experienced Assault or Harassment

Source: stopstreetharssment.org 2018 Survey:

The Privilege Problem

To understand why sexual harassment and assault are so common, we have to talk about privilege. *Privilege* refers to the special rules, powers, and advantages that certain groups enjoy in a society. In most cultures around the world, boys and men are privileged. Their privilege shows up in obvious ways, like holding more powerful jobs in business and government than women do.

But it also shows up in smaller ways. For example, studies have shown that men often interrupt women when they are speaking. They interrupt in classrooms. They interrupt in social gatherings. They interrupt in professional meetings. At first glance, interrupting women may seem unrelated to rape culture. But they are both rooted in respect for women's voices.

In our culture, a woman's voice is often considered less important than a man's voice. On TV only 25 percent of the reporters are women. We hear fewer women's voices in the music industry, in films, and on the radio. And many studies have shown that people find low-pitched male voices more trustworthy—more believable—than higher-pitched female voices.

What does it mean when we are not used to listening to women? It means that when a girl or woman says "no," it might not carry the weight that it should. It means that when a girl talks about what happened to her, she might not be trusted.

Interruptions and rape culture have something else in common. They both involve entitlement. A person who interrupts believes he is entitled to express his thoughts even though someone else is talking. A sense of entitlement

("I have a right to do what I want") is at the very heart of sexual harassment. One person feels he or she has the right to sexual contact whether or not the other person wants it. Entitlement and privilege are big parts of rape culture.

Does rape culture really exist?

We make rape or sexual assault more likely when we tolerate or minimize acts of sexual harassment, abuse, or assault. Our society minimizes or tolerates sexual misconduct in many ways and that has made sexual violence all too commonplace.

The entertainment industry presents toxic stereotypes of men and women. In books, movies, music, art, and advertising, men are depicted as dominant and aggressive. In romance films, the hero does not give up and walk away when a woman says no. He charms. He persists. He keeps up the pressure until, at last, he "wins" her.

Women, on the other hand, are often depicted as beautiful and vulnerable. In movies, books,

and music, female characters are subject to wildly changing emotions. They often need to be rescued by male characters. In addition to using stereotypes, entertainers minimize assaults against women. Comedians tell rape jokes. Musicians fondle dozens of interchangeable women in music videos. Never do they ask consent. Tabloids publish nude photos taken without a celebrity's permission. These patterns make it seem that acts of sexual aggression are *normal* and *no big deal.*

The criminal justice system also sends the message that sexual assault is not very important. Rape kits containing the DNA of rapists sit in warehouses for years without being tested. If a sexual assault does make it to trial, judges often give light sentences to boys and men who assault women. One well-known example was the 2016 trial of Brock Turner, a college student convicted of sexually assaulting an unconscious woman. In that case, judge Aaron Persky sentenced Turner to only six months in county jail, plus probation. Persky justified the sentence by saying, in part, that a lengthy prison sentence would have "a severe impact on him." Yet studies show that the effects of rape and assault can have a severe impact on survivors for many years. When a judge gives a light sentence, it sends a message that the boy's future is more important than the girl's.

Schools can also send damaging messages to girls who report abuse or assault. If a girl reports harassment, school officials sometimes say things like, "It's her word against his." They may refuse to suspend the boy or even document the event. The reasoning is that they don't want the boy's school record to be held against him in the future. Worse still, they may suspend *both* students if they cannot decide who is telling the truth. School dress codes can also reinforce rape culture. When school officials focus clothing rules on what girls wear, they imply that girls are responsible for distracting boys. They imply that boys are unable to use self-control around girls in certain styles of clothing.

Women and girls are fighting back against the idea that it is their fault if they are sexually assaulted. Assault doesn't happen because of what someone wears.

As hard as it is to admit, the problem of silencing girls even shows up in our churches, synagogues, temples, and mosques. Some religions teach girls and women to obey orders from men. Some faiths teach that girls and women must not speak against male authorities. Many enforce rigid dress codes, forcing women to cover their bodies and sometimes even their faces. When girls and women are taught to believe that resisting or reporting men is against their faith, it can lead them to keep silent about abuse.

It's Her Future Too

Sexual assault has lasting impacts on the lives of survivors. Here is a partial list of physical, emotional, and social aftereffects:

- Shaking, crying, yelling, or the complete opposite—strangely flat emotional tone
- A sense of guilt or shame
- Fear that does not go away
- Trouble sleeping
- Physical effects like muscle tension, soreness, infection, or pregnancy

More than 90 percent of survivors have post-traumatic stress disorder in the weeks after an assault. They might experience any or all of these symptoms:

- Fear, even in situations where it is not necessary
- Flashbacks and nightmares
- Trouble remembering or learning new things
- Thoughts about death or suicide
- Self-harm
- Drug or alcohol use

Studies have also shown that sexual assault can affect a survivor's education. Students who are sexually assaulted may:

- Miss school
- Have trouble studying or focusing
- Get lower grades
- Drop out of school

A 2018 study also found that sexual assault may affect survivors' health decades afterward.

Survivors of sexual assault are more likely to experience:

- Sleep disturbances
- Depression
- Anxiety
- High blood pressure

The good news is that if survivors get help early, they usually have better health later on.

What You Can Do:
Know Your Right to a Safe Environment

No matter what your gender identity, where you live, or what religion you practice, no one can legally harass, abuse, or assault you. The law is there to protect you.

Because sexual violence is everywhere in our culture, we all have to fight it wherever we can.

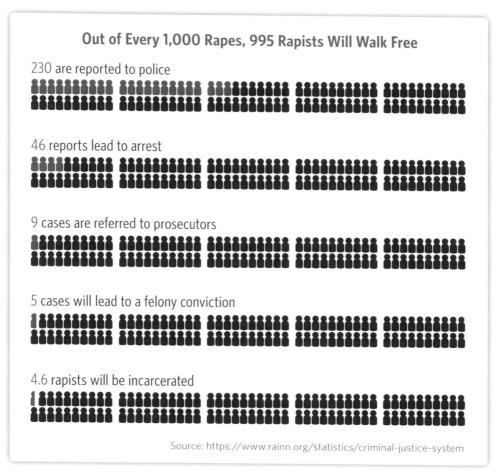

Out of Every 1,000 Rapes, 995 Rapists Will Walk Free

230 are reported to police

46 reports lead to arrest

9 cases are referred to prosecutors

5 cases will lead to a felony conviction

4.6 rapists will be incarcerated

Source: https://www.rainn.org/statistics/criminal-justice-system

CHAPTER THREE

Defying
Rape Culture

Sometimes a mighty revolution begins with a small act of resistance. The #MeToo movement began as a conversation between two teenage girls at a youth camp in Selma, Alabama. A feisty girl named Heaven revealed a painful secret to a counselor named Tarana Burke. Heaven's stepdad was doing "monstrous things" to her body. Burke tried to listen, but because she was also a survivor of sexual abuse, she could only bear to do so for a few minutes. She sent the devastated girl to find another counselor. Afterward, Burke regretted that decision.

Tarana Burke Starts #MeToo

Years later, Tarana Burke started an organization called Just Be, Inc., in Harlem, a neighborhood in New York City. She wanted to help black girls and women who had survived sexual assault. The two words that guided them: *Me, too.* The two words she wished she had been able to say to Heaven.

Burke founded an organization to make sure that black and brown girls who survived sexual assault would find a sympathetic ear. Why focus on black and brown girls? Because they are more likely to experience sexual abuse and assault than their white peers. Because their needs are often overlooked by society.

For more than 10 years, Burke's organization brought healing to women in Harlem. Then something happened on America's West Coast that made Burke's movement explode onto national headlines.

The #MeToo Revolution
Rocks the Film Industry and the World

In 2017 a shocking story hit the headlines. Famed Hollywood producer Harvey Weinstein was accused of sexually harassing multiple young women. In a detailed *New York Times* article written by journalists Jodi Kantor and Megan Twohey, several female actors said Weinstein had asked for sexual acts in exchange for roles in his films. A demand like that is an example of quid pro quo harassment. When they refused, they said, Weinstein tried to ruin their careers. A week later, a *New Yorker* article by Ronan Farrow added still more to the scandal.

In the months to come, 11 women in the U.S. accused Weinstein of everything from asking for massages to rape. Dozens of actors came forward with similar stories. Though Weinstein denied the allegations, others in the film industry took action. Movie studios canceled his projects. He was stripped of his awards and thrown out of professional organizations. In the state of New York, Weinstein would face charges of rape and sexual assault. Cases were also brought against him in the United Kingdom.

In the wake of the scandal, actor Alyssa Milano sent out this now-famous tweet:

When she sent the tweet, Milano did not know about Tarana Burke's groundbreaking work with sexual assault survivors. She found out soon afterward and gave credit to Burke:

As of October 2018, more than 19 million people had tweeted #MeToo. Burke and Milano sparked an international conversation about sexual harassment and assault. The signal boost enabled Burke and other advocates to raise money and support for programs that help survivors rebuild their lives. Since the movement went viral, Burke has traveled the world teaching, leading workshops, and building local networks to help survivors in their own communities.

Tarana Burke was a featured speaker at the 2017 Women's Convention in Detroit, Michigan. Woman after woman shared stories of the harassment and sexual assault they had experienced.

#MeToo K-12

A 2017 survey showed that 17,000 students were assaulted or harassed at school in a single five-year period in the U.S. Some people believe that number is a small fraction of the actual total. Not every student reports what happened. Not every school official documents each instance of assault. And sometimes the reports are labeled "bullying" because it's less complicated for the school.

An organization called Stop Sexual Assault in Schools (SSAIS) started a #MeTooK12 campaign. They wanted to give middle school and high school students a place to speak out about sexual assault. In addition to creating a safe space for student voices, it offers resources to kids, parents, and schools.

Time's Up: Digital Activists Take the Movement Worldwide

Following the Weinstein revelations, female actors began calling for an end to sexual harassment in the entertainment industry. Their rallying cry was "Time's Up," meaning sexual harassment would no longer be tolerated. These women simply wanted to work without being harassed. They wanted the same pay as male actors. And they wanted industry leaders to be publicly called out for bad behavior.

To signal their support of the Time's Up cause, many women wore all black at the Golden Globes and carried

In honor of Time's Up, actors (left to right) Laura Dern, Nicole Kidman, Zoe Kravitz, Reese Witherspoon, Shailene Woodley, and many others wore black to the 2018 Golden Globes.

white roses at the Grammys. Working together, they raised more than $22 million for a legal defense fund at the National Women's Law Center. They wanted women who had little money to be able to fight their harassers in court. As of early 2019, almost 800 lawyers had volunteered to help.

The Time's Up movement has led to the downfall of more than 200 business leaders, music executives, comedians, actors, and news anchors whose sexual misconduct was once winked at. There is hardly an industry that hasn't felt shock waves.

Spotlight on a Fighter:
Mona Eltahawy and #MosqueMeToo

When Mona Eltahawy was 15, she traveled to Mecca, Saudi Arabia. Her journey was part of a holy pilgrimage called the Hajj. As she prayed in the crowded mosque, a man grabbed her behind and refused to let go. It was a horrible to be violated—worse, it happened in a space dedicated to her faith. She cried. And kept the assault secret.

Eltahawy, who is now a journalist, eventually realized she was not alone. Many young women were groped during the Hajj. Most of them never reported what happened to them. They kept quiet because the subject of sexual assault is taboo. To create a safe space for Muslim girls and women to report, she started the #MosqueMeToo campaign. In less than 24 hours, more than 2,000 women had shared their stories. It went on to become one of the top 10 trends on Twitter in the Farsi language.

#MuteRKelly

In addition to sparking social change on a national level, some of the entertainment industry's most notorious individuals have been exposed on social media. Since the 1990s, accusations of sexual abuse and violence have dogged R&B musician Robert Kelly. Many of the accusations involve the abuse of underage girls. Kelly has always denied the allegations, and in 2008 a Chicago jury found him not guilty of child pornography charges.

Over the past 20 years, however, many of his former girlfriends have told similar stories of forced sex, extreme control, and violence. Some young women have said he keeps "his girls" in a cultlike environment, telling them when to eat and what to wear. To keep them isolated, they say, he does not let them talk to their families. And when they break his rules, the women say that he hits and chokes them.

In 2018 two determined activists said, "Enough." Kenyette Barnes and Oronike Odeleye began the campaign #MuteRKelly. Their goal was to persuade radio stations and concert venues to stop supporting the singer. Some of Kelly's fans who believe he is innocent have supported him publicly. Little by little, however, the #MuteRKelly campaign gained ground. Many concerts were canceled. A number of streaming services stopped offering his music. Tarana Burke, founder of the #MeToo movement, reached out to radio host Tom Joyner, whose station is broadcast nationwide. He agreed to stop playing Kelly's music.

Burke said, "We have to question what is more valuable, the lives and livelihood and wholeness and healthiness of black women and girls or some music? It's not just about playing his music; it's about supporting him in ways that keep him wealthy so that he can continue to prey on black women."

In 2019 the Lifetime television network aired a six-part documentary called *Surviving R. Kelly*. The film features numerous former Kelly "girlfriends" who describe horrific abuse. A few weeks afterward, Kelly was dropped by RCA, his record label. In February 2019, Kelly was charged with 10 counts of criminal sex abuse involving four women, three of whom were underage. His lawyer maintains his innocence.

Online and on the ground, girls and women began speaking out, standing by one another, and holding people accountable for their actions.

Some have focused on the number of people brought down by recent activism. But Tarana Burke and millions of survivors and advocates insist that the #MeToo movement is not about perpetrators. It's about survivors. In Burke's words, the movement is about "empowerment through empathy."

> ## Fact
>
> In 2017 *Time* magazine's Person of the Year was not a single person, but a group of daring whistleblowers. The magazine dubbed them "The Silence Breakers." These women and men bravely spoke out about harassment they endured in a wide range of industries.

In a 2018 TED talk, Tarana Burke said, "We owe future generations a world free of sexual violence. I believe we can build that world."

#MeToo Forces Out Government Officials

This chart shows the status of 138 public officials accused of sexual misconduct during the 2016–2018 election cycle. What does this chart show about the effect the #MeToo movement is having on our culture?

- 25% remain in office
- 75% out of office

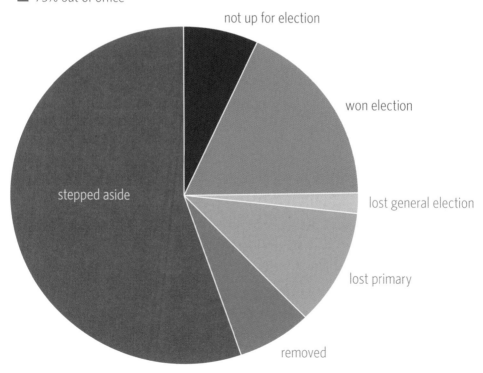

not up for election

won election

lost general election

stepped aside

lost primary

removed

Source: https://www.law.georgetown.edu/wp-content/uploads/2018/11/MeToo-and-Public-Officials.pdf

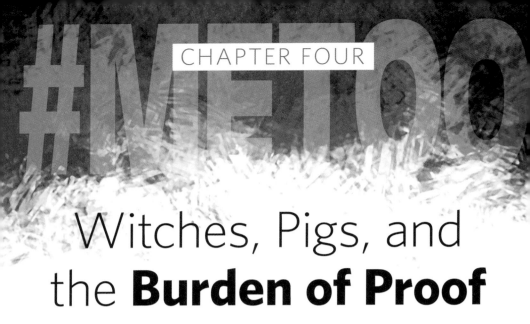

CHAPTER FOUR

Witches, Pigs, and the **Burden of Proof**

Not everyone is happy about the effects of the #MeToo movement. Criticism of the movement falls into several categories.

"This has become a witch hunt."

Some critics of the #MeToo movement say that innocent men are being punished along with the guilty. The U.S. Constitution says that no person should be "deprived of life, liberty, or property without due process." That means every accused person is entitled to a thorough investigation and fair evaluation of the facts by whatever authority is in charge.

Critics say that we shouldn't automatically believe everyone who makes an accusation. They point to the problem of false reports. False reports do sometimes happen. But when researchers analyze reports of sexual assault, they find that only 2 to 10 percent of reports turn out to be false. That means 90 to 98 percent of the time, people reporting sexual assault are telling the truth. Because of the likelihood that the accuser is telling the truth *and* to protect the rights of the innocent, it is important to focus on thoroughly investigating every report.

Fact

The phrase "witch hunt" refers to the Salem Witch Trials, which took place in Massachusetts in the 1690s. Puritan leaders executed about 20 young women they found guilty of practicing witchcraft. Colony leaders later admitted they had made a terrible mistake.

The problem of protecting both the innocent and the accused is especially difficult on college campuses. Title IX is the law that governs equal access to education for people of all genders. From time to time since the law was passed in 1972, the Department of Education (DOE) has issued "guidance" letters explaining what schools should do to protect students' rights. In 2011 the Obama administration expanded the definition of harassment. It also made it easier to prove that sexual harassment had taken place.

The DOE under President Trump did away with those requirements. One of the DOE's concerns is that making harassment easier to prove would violate the due process rights of accused students. Under the Trump-era guidance, schools can use an older standard of proof—"clear and convincing evidence"—instead of the more recent, much higher level of proof, "preponderance of the evidence."

"#MeToo is making it hard for men to date or relate to women in the workplace."

Some critics of the #MeToo movement worry that it will kill "office romance." In France, the movement #BalanceTonPorc ("Call out your pig") is the #MeToo equivalent. But critics of the movement in France say that it has gone too far.

One hundred female French artists and actors who are against #BalanceTonPorc signed an open letter against it. The signers urged people not to mix up rape and "seduction." The letter was published in the French newspaper *Le Monde*.

Some people also worry that women will pay a professional price for changes in the workplace. Men might not want to mentor, promote, travel with, or meet after hours with women coworkers. Why not? Because, some people say, men will fear being accused of harassment. And if men react that way, it may cost women important opportunities.

Some business leaders say the solution is to make access equal. If male executives don't feel comfortable having dinner with female coworkers, they shouldn't have dinner with male colleagues either.

"#MeToo is leaving out women of color and women in low-wage jobs."

One of the most important criticisms of the movement is that its focus has shifted to the famous and fortunate. It's a double-edged sword. Celebrities with massive Twitter followings bring attention to the problem. They can also raise money to provide services for survivors. But their fame can also draw the focus away from women of color and people in low-wage jobs—people at higher risk for exploitation in the first place. Advocates are also concerned about the harassment experienced by the 12 million immigrant women working in the U.S. today. For them, reporting sexual harassment carries an additional risk: deportation.

In a 2017 *Washington Post* article, #MeToo founder Tarana Burke wrote, "What history has shown us time and again is that if marginalized voices—those of people of color, queer people, disabled people, poor people—aren't centered in our movements then they tend to become no more than a footnote. I often say that sexual violence knows no race, class or gender, but the response to it does."

For the present, Burke and other advocates are taking advantage of the #MeToo movement to raise funds to get resources to communities that are often ignored. And some lawmakers are working to expand legal protections to include everyone, even undocumented workers.

Seeds of Change

Support for the Time's Up movement came from across the nation. The Alianza Nacional de Campesinas, an association of farmworker families, sent this letter to the movement's organizers:

> Dear Sisters,
> We write on behalf of the approximately 700,000 women who work in the agricultural fields and packing sheds across the United States. For the past several weeks we have watched and listened with sadness as we have learned of the actors, models and other individuals who have come forward to speak out about the gender based violence they've experienced at the hands of bosses, coworkers and other powerful people in the entertainment industry. We wish that we could say we're shocked to learn that this is such a pervasive problem in your industry. Sadly, we're not surprised because it's a reality we know far too well. Countless farmworker women across our

country suffer in silence because of the widespread sexual harassment and assault that they face at work.

We do not work under bright stage lights or on the big screen. We work in the shadows of society in isolated fields and packinghouses that are out of sight and out of mind for most people in this country. Your job feeds souls, fills hearts and spreads joy. Our job nourishes the nation with the fruits, vegetables and other crops that we plant, pick and pack.

Even though we work in very different environments, we share a common experience of being preyed upon by individuals who have the power to hire, fire, blacklist and otherwise threaten our economic, physical and emotional security. Like you, there are few positions available to us and reporting any kind of harm or injustice committed against us doesn't seem like a viable option. Complaining about anything—even sexual harassment—seems unthinkable because too much is at risk, including the ability to feed our families and preserve our reputations.

We understand the hurt, confusion, isolation and betrayal that you might feel. We also carry shame and fear resulting from this violence. It sits on our backs like oppressive weights. But, deep in our hearts we know that it is not our fault. The only people at fault are the individuals who choose to abuse their power to harass, threaten and harm us, like they have harmed you.

In these moments of despair, and as you cope with scrutiny and criticism because you have bravely chosen to speak out against the harrowing acts that were committed against you, please know that you're not alone. We believe and stand with you.

In solidarity,

Alianza Nacional de Campesinas

What You Can Do: Know Your Rights

You can ask your school administrators to post or publish your school's procedures for making a sexual assault complaint. Find out if your school has a designated point person for reporting. And you can educate yourself about your right to file a complaint outside your school district if necessary. Visit knowyourix.org to learn about your rights.

Race and Industry Affect Sexual Harassment

As a national conversation continues to take place about sexual harassment, an analysis by the National Women's Law Center of EEOC complaints filed between 2012 and 2016 found that race and industry appeared to play key roles in how likely women in the private sector were to experience such treatment on the job.

 More than **1 in 3** (35.8%) **women** who filed charges alleging sexual harassment also alleged retaliation.

And **1 in 17** (5.8%) **women** also alleged discrimination based on race.

 Per 100,000 women workers, **black women** filed sexual harassment charges with the EEOC at nearly **3 times** the rate of white, non-Hispanic women.

In every industry, black women are disproportionately represented among women who filed sexual harassment charges. Some of the industries with the highest number of complaints were: food services, retail trade, hotels, health care/social assistance, and manufacturing.

Generation X (born 1965-1979) and Millennial (1980-1996) women both filed more sexual harassment charges with the EEOC than Baby Boomer (1946-1964) women.

Nearly 6 in 10 (58.9%) sexual harassment charges filed with the EEOC between 2012 and 2016 failed to list an industry, making it impossible to tell the industry where the alleged harassment occurred.

43.9 percent of those who filed sexual harassment complaints worked for small businesses with 15 to 100 workers.

Source: National Women's Law Center

CHAPTER FIVE

Boundaries, Blame, and **Bystanders**

Permanently dismantling rape culture will not be achieved with hashtags, memes, and angry updates. New behaviors, based on mutual respect, must replace toxic traditions.

Changing the Habit of Victim-Blaming

Until very recently, discussions about rape have often focused on how people—usually girls—can avoid it. *Don't wear your shorts too short or your jeans too tight. Don't smile too much. Stay out of nightclubs and dark alleys. Don't drink alcohol or go to parties.*

There's nothing wrong with paying attention to good safety advice. But the victims of sexual assault are not the problem. The problem is the people who sexually assault. When we focus advice on what people can do to avoid assault, it's almost as if we are saying, "If you had behaved differently, this would not have happened to you."

That idea is known as "victim-blaming." Victim-blaming can make people keep quiet about what has happened to them. It is a tactic used to excuse criminals for what they've done. Victim-blaming can sound like this:

- "If she was really raped, why did she wait so long to report it?"
- "With that outfit, she was asking for it."
- "Why didn't she fight back?"
- "If she didn't want to have sex, why did she go to the party/drink too much/go to his dorm room, etc.?"

All of these questions make the survivor responsible for someone else's actions. In real life, there is no such thing as "asking for it." The only person responsible for rape is the rapist.

Victim-blaming can be subtle. Sometimes, people use what is known as the "passive voice" to write about sexual assault. For example, people say, "She was raped." The sentence does not assign any blame to the rapist, who is not mentioned at all. If we say, "He raped her," we are writing in an active voice. Someone in the sentence is responsible for raping her. Instead of asking, "How many students *are assaulted* in school every year?" we can ask, "How many times does *someone assault* a student in school every year?" This may seem like a small shift, but it signals a big change in attitude.

Girls' Responses to Being Harassed or Assaulted

This chart shows that people respond to being assaulted in many ways. Which ways surprise you? Can you see why it is important not to judge someone for how they respond to assault?

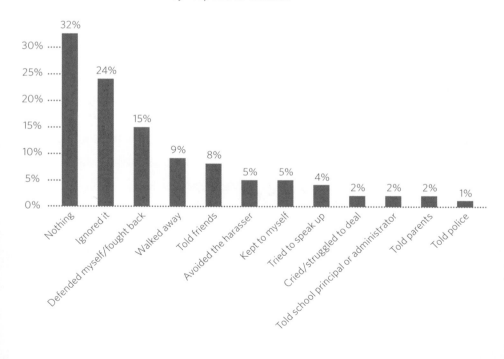

Source: National Women's Law Center, Let Her Learn Survey, Conducted by Lake Research Partners (2017).

When we build our sentences to focus on the victims rather than on the perpetrators, we are helping to hide the perpetrators. We are using language that does not hold those who commit assault accountable for what they do.

Educating Everyone about Consent

Before any kind of sexual contact takes place, both people must agree that it is okay. That means both people must *clearly, verbally consent* to the activity. The first step in getting consent is to ask. One person cannot presume to know what someone else wants. We have to ask, every time, even when it feels awkward.

The second step is to listen. If a person does not say "yes," then the activity must not occur or continue.

Fact

Consent means that both parties agree to the activity. Consent must be clear. It must be ongoing. It must be free and voluntary.

Consent cannot happen if:

- Someone is drunk, drugged, mentally disabled, sleeping, or unconscious
- Someone is younger than the legal age of consent (which varies from state to state)
- Someone is in a powerful position, such as in a teacher-student or coach-player relationship
- Someone feels afraid or forced

If a person says, "no," "not now," "maybe some other time," or "I don't know," they have not consented.

The third step is to respect the other person's decision. Trying to persuade, pressure, or charm the other person into doing what you want violates that person's rights. It is also important to keep asking throughout the encounter. Saying yes to a kiss doesn't mean a person has consented to something else. People have the right to change their minds at any point.

Learning about Non-Verbal Cues

When you are involved in any activity with other people, it's important to notice their gestures, facial expressions, and body language. If someone tenses, freezes, stops smiling, pulls back, or does anything to signal that something has changed, stop. Ask how the other person is feeling. If you notice changes in your own body—anxiety, sweating, fast heartbeats, shaking—it is okay to take a break. Those physical clues may mean that you do not want to continue. If you have changed your mind, it is okay to say so.

Not everyone is good at reading body language. People tend to get better at reading another person's body language the longer they know each other.

Whether it is your first date or your 10th, your first kiss or your 50th, consent is not a onetime agreement. Keep making sure you have an enthusiastic, verbal yes.

Turning Bystanders into Upstanders

Say you're on a bus, in a hallway, or online. Suddenly, someone makes a rude sexual remark. Someone grabs or gropes or posts something they shouldn't. What do you do? Figuring out when, where, and how to interrupt can be tricky. If you're a girl, you may not want to become a target of abuse yourself. If you're a boy, you may not want to defy unwritten "bro codes" that say guys should stick together.

Studies show that only 30 percent of bystanders get involved when they see sexual harassment taking place. Most of them say they just didn't know what to do.

Writers at *Teen Vogue* magazine recommend several ways to become an upstander instead of a bystander. You can distract. You can delegate. Or you can be direct. To distract, you could speak to the person who is being targeted. Show her something on your phone or ask to borrow something. Your goal is to interrupt the situation before it gets worse.

What Makes Kids Intervene?

This chart is based on a study conducted by school safety researchers at Georgia State University. It shows what makes people step in and try to stop bullying. What three things can you learn from it about interrupting sexual harassment or assault?

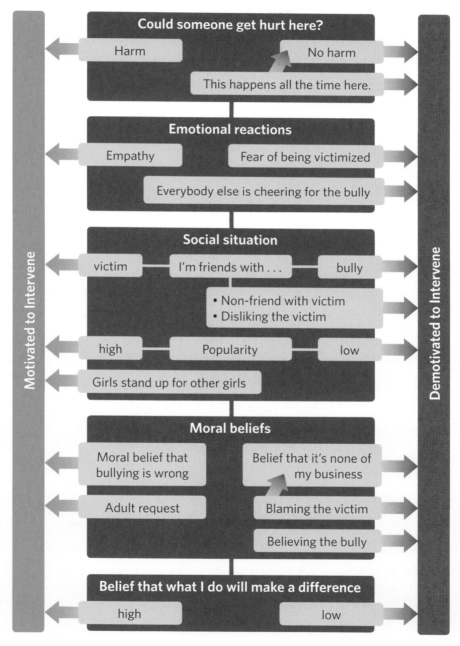

Source: Georgia State University

You can also delegate by asking someone else to help you intervene. You could go get an adult. You could ask someone else to speak up with you.

Finally, if you feel it is safe, you can step in and be direct. Tell the harasser that what he or she is doing is wrong. Try to remove the targeted person from the situation. It's important to be sure, though, that you are safe yourself. It may seem like a small thing to step in and show someone a gif during a tense moment. But it is a very big deal to the person who is being harassed.

Reimagining Masculinity

Most men are not rapists. But most rapists are men. If we want a world free of sexual violence, we need to ask ourselves if what we are teaching boys about their place in the world makes rape more likely. We need to look at some of the messages boys get about what it means to "be a man."

Think about what it means to be a "good man." You might think a good man is one who is:

- Caring
- Honest
- Puts the needs of other people first

Now think about what it means to be a "real man." If you think about the way "real men" are portrayed in media, you might say a real man:

- Takes charge
- Takes risks
- Never cries

Our society sends boys confusing messages about manhood. In movies and video games, heroic men have ripped, muscular bodies. They never give up on their quests. If women are present, their job is to glorify, to watch, to be rescued. Our culture teaches us that aggression, strength, persistence, and domination are manly qualities. Beauty, silence, and vulnerability are seen as ideal in women.

Watching or playing violent video games can reinforce ideals of men as warriors.

These are extreme examples, of course. But they are all around us. And some researchers think these stereotypes contribute to rape culture.

What You Can Do:
Pay Attention to Boundaries

Every one of us has the right to decide what happens to our bodies. You do not have to explain or defend your limits to anyone. And no one else should have to defend or explain their limits to you. Sometimes we don't know why we feel uncomfortable. We just do. And that is enough reason to say no.

It can be hard to say no if you have been trained from childhood that other people have the right to hug or kiss you. It can be even harder if you have been trained that it is your job to please other people. If you have been raised to be polite and to try to make others happy, saying no may feel upsetting. The best thing you can do is learn to recognize and respect your own boundaries.

It might be hard to accept "no" from someone when you want to keep going. It can be harder if you have been raised to think that if you keep trying, you will eventually get what you want. That idea may be useful when it comes to academics or athletics, but it leads to problems when it is applied to sex or relationships. When someone says no or draws a boundary, the best thing you can do is respect it.

CHAPTER SIX

Vote and Promote:
Empowering Women

A child awakens in the morning. She dresses for school without worrying whether her outfit will make someone call her names. In homeroom, she talks with other students, girls and boys, fearlessly. In each class, she turns in homework. She was able to complete it with a clear, focused mind. In the hallway and on the bus ride home, no one bothers her.

This is the world that every student deserves. Even with the awakening caused by the #MeToo movement, we are not there yet. What can we do to keep moving forward? We can empower girls and women so that the balance of power in the world is more equal. Here are some steps we can take to equalize power in our culture.

Believe Survivors

One of the most persistent myths in rape culture is the idea that people often make up stories of sexual assault. Decades of research show that most reports of sexual assault are true. So the most important thing we can do to empower survivors is simply to believe them.

A person who has gone through the trauma of sexual assault needs comfort and understanding.

Put Women in Charge

Sexual assault and rape are not about sex. They are about power. Research shows us that when women are in charge, sexual harassment in the workplace drops. Workplace sexual harassment also decreases when women are not vastly outnumbered by men.

Women in Leadership in the United States

Look at this series of charts on women in leadership. Does this information seem hopeful?

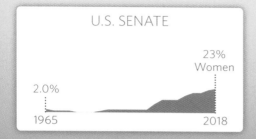

U.S. SENATE

2.0%
1965

23%
Women
2018

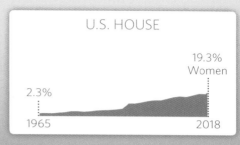

U.S. HOUSE

2.3%
1965

19.3%
Women
2018

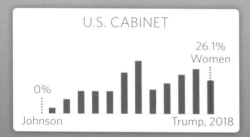

U.S. CABINET

0%
Johnson

26.1%
Women
Trump, 2018

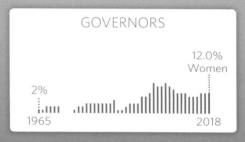

GOVERNORS

2%
1965

12.0%
Women
2018

STATE LEGISLATURES

4.5%
1971

25.4%
Women
2018

FORTUNE 500 CEOs

0%
1995

4.8%
Women
2018

Source: Pew Research Center

Let Girls and Women Learn

Across the globe, more than 130 million girls are not in school, and about 15 million of them never will be. When girls are not educated, their families, villages, and nations suffer. Research shows that educating girls raises their income. Education improves their health. It strengthens the economy where they live. Education also makes them less likely to experience sexual violence.

Learning is power.
Educating girls improves the world.

Celebrate Survivors Everywhere

There was once a time when survivors of sexual abuse suffered in silence. There were few safe spaces where they could talk about what happened. Many felt isolated. But now the number of spaces where people can share their experiences is exploding. People share their stories in online forums and support groups. They join other survivors in art, yoga, and dance studios with special programs for them. They speak out in memoirs and poetry slams. They march alongside other survivors in protests all across the nation.

Jewish Students Create a Feminist Seder

Last year, a small group of Jewish teenagers in the Chicago area wrote a Passover service to teach others about rape culture in their community.

In the Jewish tradition, the Passover seder celebrates the escape of the Jews from slavery in Egypt. One seat at the family table is left empty in honor of the biblical prophet Elijah. To honor survivors of sexual assault, these students reserve an empty seat at their table for Dinah instead of Elijah. In the Bible, Dinah is raped by a local prince. In honoring Dinah and other survivors, they are making their religious traditions their own.

In the year since the #MeToo movement took Twitter by storm, a worldwide conversation about sexual assault has opened up. The Nobel Peace Prize was awarded to Nadia Murad and Denis Mukwege, two brave activists who fight sexual violence in war zones. And women all over the world have united to tell their stories. They are confronting powerful abusers and empathizing with one another.

Nadia Murad and Denis Mukwege received the Nobel Peace Prize for their efforts to end the use of sexual violence as a weapon of war.

To date, the #MeToo movement has spread to dozens of countries. In some places, it's a mere upsurge in Twitter activity. In others, it's part of widespread social change.

Just as there were heroes in the fight for women's voting rights, there are heroes all over the world in the fight against sexual violence. Every survivor who reaches out for help and healing. Every investigator who digs deep to find

A Gymnastic Feat

In August 2016 Rachel Denhollander sent an email to reporters at the *IndyStar*, an Indiana newspaper. She told them that when she was 15 years old, she was sexually assaulted by Larry Nassar. Nassar was a doctor for USA Gymnastics. Her brave story led to an investigation. By the time of his trial, more than 150 other survivors had come forward. He had been molesting young gymnasts and other girls for nearly 30 years. Nassar was convicted and sentenced to 175 years in prison.

When judge Rosemarie Aquilina handed down her sentence, she said to Denhollander, "You made all of these voices matter. Your sister survivors and I thank you. You are the bravest person I've ever had in my courtroom."

Fellow gymnast Aly Raisman was one of the many young women who gave impact statements at Nassar's trial. She said, "My dream is that one day everyone will know what the words MeToo signify, but they will be educated and able to protect themselves from predators like Larry, so that they will never, ever, ever have to say the words, 'Me, too.'"

Aly Raisman (left) was one of more than 150 current and former gymnasts who gave evidence about Larry Nassar's abuse. She also spoke out in the media to tell the world what he had done.

out the truth. Every educator who explains consent. Every ally who sits beside an abused friend. Those who confront. Those who support. Those who survive.

In the age of #MeToo, every one of us has the responsibility to change the culture that enables sexual harassment and sexual violence to take place. It is our world to reimagine and recreate.

GET INVOLVED

If Someone You Know Has Been Assaulted:

Listen without judging.

It takes a lot of courage to talk about assault. If your friend has trusted you with this information, let her know you believe her.

Tell her it's not her fault.

Tell your friend she is not to blame even if she feels guilt or shame. Try not to ask questions that might make her feel that she has done something wrong. Instead of asking, "Why didn't you scream?" say, "You did not do anything to cause this."

Don't make it about you.

If your friend's story reminds you of something you have gone through, it's good to show empathy. You might say, "You are not alone. I'm right here with you." But share your own experiences another time.

Explore resources.

If your friend is ready to report what happened, offer to be there in support. If possible, look up the contact information for local organizations that offer help to survivors.

Take care of yourself.

When someone you love tells you about an assault, you might feel angry, sad, afraid, or shocked. Be gentle with yourself and get help if you need it. The same resources available to your friend are also available for you.

MYTHS ABOUT RAPE

Myth: Girls say no, but mean yes.

Fact: Consent is a freely given, clearly stated "yes." Silence is not consent. Being drunk or drugged and unable to understand or speak is not consent. Being passed out or unconscious is not consent.

Myth: If she had sex with me before, she has consented to have sex with me again.

Fact: Previous sexual conduct, including previous consent to sex, is not consent to sex right now. If she kissed you yesterday, that doesn't mean she wants to kiss you today.

Myth: Victims provoke rape when they dress provocatively, act sexy, go to someone's room or house or a bar.

Fact: Rape is never the victim's fault. It is a crime of violence and control that stems from the perpetrator's determination to exercise power over another. Neither a person's clothing nor behavior are invitations for unwanted sexual activity. Forcing someone to engage in nonconsensual sexual activity is rape, regardless of the way that person dresses or acts.

Myth: It's not rape if it happens after drinking or taking drugs.

Fact: A person under the influence of drugs or alcohol can't consent to sexual activity. If consent isn't given, it is rape.

Myth: Most rapes are committed by strangers. It's not rape if the people involved knew each other.

Fact: Most rapes are committed by someone the victim knows. For both completed and attempted rapes, about 8 in 10 offenders were known to the victim. Rape can be committed within any type of relationship, including marriage and dating. People can be raped by classmates, acquaintances, or coworkers.

Myth: A person who has really been raped will be hysterical.

Fact: Being raped is a very traumatic experience. Victims of sexual violence exhibit a variety of responses to the assault, which can include: calmness, hysteria, withdrawal, anger, apathy, denial, and shock. Reactions to the rape and the length of time needed to heal from the trauma vary with each person. There is no "right way" to react to a rape.

Myth: All rape victims will report the crime immediately to the police. If they do not report it or delay in reporting it, then they must not have been raped. Either they made up the story because they're mad at their boyfriend or they're trying to stay out of trouble with their parents or they want to extort money from the guy.

Fact: There are many reasons why a rape victim may not report the assault to the police. Only three in 10 rapes are reported to law enforcement. It is not easy to talk about being raped. The experience of retelling what happened may cause the person to relive the trauma. Other reasons for not immediately reporting the assault, or not reporting it at all, include fear of retaliation by the offender, fear of not being believed, fear of being blamed for the assault, fear of being "revictimized." If the case goes through the criminal justice system, the victim may believe that the offender will not be held accountable. Not recognizing that what happened was rape, shame, and/or shock are other reasons for not reporting.

Myth: Only young, pretty women are raped.

Fact: Anyone can be raped.

Source:

GLOSSARY

feminist—someone who believes strongly that women ought to have the same opportunities and rights that men have

lynching—putting to death, often by hanging, by mob action and without legal authority

perpetrate—to bring about or carry out something, such as a crime

privilege—special status, protections, or powers in a culture

probation—the early release of a prisoner under certain conditions

rape—penetration of another person's body without consent

sexual assault—any sexual act performed without consent

sexual harassment—unwelcome sexual advances, whether verbal or physical

Title IX—the section of the Equal Rights Act that prohibits gender-based discrimination

trauma—an experience that is either deeply emotionally upsetting or physically wounding

ADDITIONAL RESOURCES

Critical Thinking Questions

Do you think girls should have dress codes? What about boys? Explain why you think some school authorities focus more on dress codes than behavior.

Your friend sends you an inappropriate picture of his girlfriend. What could you say or do to make it clear that you don't think what he is doing is right? Is it enough just to delete the picture? Should you say something in person or online? What if you're pretty sure speaking up will hurt your friendship?

What are some things you could ask to be sure you have permission to touch another person?

Further Reading

Leigh, Anna. *Aly Raisman: Athlete and Activist.* Minneapolis, MN: Lerner Publishing, 2019.

Stanley, Debbie. *Everything You Need to Know About Student-on-Student Sexual Harassment.* New York: Rosen Publishing, 2000.

Internet Sites

How to Be a Good Friend
teenvogue.com/story/best-friend-sexual-assault-survivor

Let Her Learn: Stopping School Pushout
nwlc-ciw49tixgw5lbab.stackpathdns.com/wp-content/

The National Sexual Assault Hotline
rainn.org/about-national-sexual-assault-telephone-hotline

Preventing Teen Sexual Assault
safebae.org

SOURCE NOTES

p. 4, "I went up a narrow flight of stairs…" Transcript of Christine Blasey-Ford's testimony before the Senate Judiciary Committee, January 26, 2018, https://www.judiciary.senate.gov/imo/media/doc/09-27-18%20Ford%20Testimony.pdf Accessed February 6, 2019.

p. 10, "high-tech lynching…" Transcript of Judge Clarence Thomas's testimony before the Senate Judiciary Committee, American Rhetoric, October 11, 1991, https://www.americanrhetoric.com/speeches/clarencethomashightechlynching.htm. Accessed February 6, 2019.

p. 16, "a severe impact on him…" "Stanford Sexual Assault Case," *The Guardian*, June 14, 2016, https://www.theguardian.com/us-news/2016/jun/14/stanford-sexual-assault-read-sentence-judge-aaron-persky Accessed December 29, 2018.

p. 20, "monstrous things…" Tarana Burke, "The Inception," Just Be Inc., 2018, http://justbeinc.wixsite.com/justbeinc/the-me-too-movement-cmml Accessed February 6, 2019.

p. 22, "If you've been…" Alyssa Milano, Twitter, https://twitter.com/alyssa_milano/status/919659438700670976?lang=en Accessed March 25, 2019.

p. 22, "I was just made aware…" Alyssa Milano, Twitter, https://twitter.com/alyssa_milano/status/920067975016624128?lang=en Accessed March 25, 2019.

p. 28, "We have to question…." Jessica Bennett, "Tom Joyner Now Refusing to Play R. Kelly's Music on Radio Show," *Ebony*, April 26, 2018, https://www.ebony.com/entertainment/tom-joyner-refusing-play-r-kelly-music/ Accessed February 6, 2019.

p. 28, " We owe future…" Tarana Burke, "MeToo Is a Movement, Not a Moment," TED, 2018, https://www.ted.com/talks/tarana_burke_me_too_is_a_movement_not_a_moment?language=en Accessed December 29, 2018.

p. 34, "What history has shown…" Tarana Burke, "MeToo was started for black and brown women and girls. They're still being ignored," *The Washington Post*, November 9, 2017, https://www.washingtonpost.com/news/post-nation/wp/2017/11/09/the-waitress-who-works-in-the-diner-needs-to-know-that-the-issue-of-sexual-harassment-is-about-her-too/?utm_term=.16b907f93329 Accessed February 6, 2019.

p. 53, "You made all…" Harriet Agerholm, "Rachel Denhollander: Abused US gymnast receives standing ovation in court after judge's tribute to her courage," *The Independent*, January 25, 2018, https://www.independent.co.uk/news/world/americas/rachael-denhollander-standing-ovation-video-larry-nassar-judge-aquilina-praise-a8177456.html Accessed February 6, 2019.

p. 53, "My dream is that…" Full Text of Aly Raisman's Statement, *The New York Times*, January 20, 2018, https://www.nytimes.com/2018/01/20/sports/full-text-of-aly-raismans-statement.html Accessed February 6, 2019.

SELECT BIBLIOGRAPHY

Books

Harding, Kate. *Asking for It: The Alarming Rise of Rape Culture—and What We Can Do about It.* Boston: Da Capo Lifelong Books, 2015.

Prout, Chessy. *I Have the Right To: A High School Survivor's Story of Sexual Assault, Justice, and Hope.* New York: Margaret K. McElderry Books, 2018.

Soloway, Jill. *She Wants It: Desire, Power, and Toppling the Patriarchy.* New York: Crown Archetype, 2018.

Films

Mock, Freida Lee, *Anita*, directed by Freida Lee Mock, released March 21, 2014.

Simmons, Tamara, et al., *Surviving R. Kelly*, Lifetime Network, 2019.

Websites and Articles

Bucar, Liz, and Amanda Randone, "This Woman Is Giving a Voice to Muslims in the #MeToo Movement," *Teen Vogue*, June 26, 2018, https://www.teenvogue.com/story/this-woman-is-giving-a-voice-to-muslims-in-the-metoo-movement Accessed March 9, 2019.

"Child Sexual Abuse Fact Sheet," National Child Traumatic Stress Network, 2009, https://www.nctsn.org/sites/default/files/resources//child_sexual_abuse_fact_sheet_parents_teachers_caregivers.pdf Accessed March 9, 2019.

Dobbin, Frank, and Alexandra Kalev, "Training Programs and Reporting Systems Won't End Sexual Harassment. Promoting More Women Will." *Harvard Business Review*, November 15, 2017, https://hbr.org/2017/11/training-programs-and-reporting-systems-wont-end-sexual-harassment-promoting-more-women-will Accessed March 9, 2019.

Eltahawy, Mona, "What the World Would Look Like If We Taught Girls Rage," NBC News, February 1, 2018, https://www.nbcnews.com/think/opinion/what-world-would-look-if-we-taught-girls-rage-ncna843511 Accessed March 9, 2019.

Filcman, Debra, "These teenage girls are leading an exodus from rape culture this Passover," *Chicago Reader*, March 27, 2018, https://www.chicagoreader.com/chicago/passover-haggadah-seder-rape-culture/Content?oid=44115963 Accessed March 9, 2019.

Gutierrez, Angelica, "This La Salle Bacolod Student is Fighting Rape Culture Through Art," *Esquire*, March 20, 2018, https://www.esquiremag.ph/culture/arts-and-entertainment/this-la-salle-bacolod-student-is-fighting-rape-culture-through-art-a00225-20180320 Accessed March 9, 2019.

Ilies, Remus, et al., "Reported incidence rates of work-related sexual harassment in the United States: Using meta-analysis to explain reported rate disparities," Research Gate, December 2006, https://www.researchgate.net/publication/227604263_Reported_incidence_rates_of_work-related_sexual_harassment_in_the_United_States_Using_meta-analysis_to_explain_reported_rate_disparities Accessed March 9, 2019.

Kessler-Harris, Alice, "The Long History of Workplace Sexual Harassment," *Jacobin*, https://www.jacobinmag.com/2018/03/metoo-workplace-discrimination-sexual-harassment-feminism Accessed March 9, 2019.

Mentors in Violence Prevention, http://www.mvpstrat.com/mvp-programs/high-school/ Accessed March 9, 2019.

"#MeToo Pushes Government Officials Out," https://www.law.georgetown.edu/wp-content/uploads/2018/11/MeToo-and-Public-Officials.pdf Accessed March 25, 2019.

"Race and Class Impact Sexual Harrassment," www.nwlc.org, Accessed March 25, 2019.

"Scope of the Problem: Statistics," https://www.rainn.org/statistics/scope-problem" Accessed March 25, 2019.

"The Healthy Sex Talk: Teaching Kids Consent, Ages 1–21," The Good Men Project, March 20, 2013, https://goodmenproject.com/families/the-healthy-sex-talk-teaching-kids-consent-ages-1-21/ Accessed March 9, 2019.

Thornberg, Robert, et al., "Bystander Motivation in Bullying Incidents: To Intervene or Not to Intervene?" *Western Journal of Emergency Medicine*, August 13, 2012, https://www.ncbi.nlm.nih.gov/pmc/articles/PMC3415829/ Accessed March 9, 2019.

"Want to Prevent Harassment and Assault in Schools? Listen to Students," National Education Association, November 19, 2018, http://neatoday.org/2018/11/19/want-to-prevent-harassment-and-assault-in-schools-listen-to-students/ Accessed March 9, 2019.

"Women in Leadership in the U.S.," Pew Research Center, http://www.pewsocialtrends.org/fact-sheet/the-data-on-women-leaders/ Accessed March 25, 2019.

About the Author

Rebecca Stanborough is a writer and teacher dedicated to empowering young people. She has a Master of Fine Arts in Writing for Children and Young Adults from Hamline University. *Sexual Harassment in the Age of #MeToo* is her sixth book for young readers.

INDEX